A Kid's Guide to CHINA

Jack L. Roberts

Curious Kids Press • Palm Springs, CA
www.curiouskidspress.com

Publisher: *Curious Kids Press, Palm Springs, CA 92264.*
Editor: *Sterling Moss*
Designed by: *Michael Owens*
Copy Editor: *Janice Ross*

Table of Contents

Welcome to China

Photo: *A Chinese Guardian Lion statue stands guard at the entrance to the inner palace at The Forbidden City in Beijing.*

HOW WOULD YOU LIKE to take a ride on the fastest train in the world? It goes 268 mph (431 km/h).

Or maybe you would like to take a walk on the longest wall in the world. It's more than 5,500 miles (8851 km) long.

How about climbing the tallest mountain some day? It's called Mount Everest and it's 20,029 feet (8,843 m) tall at its peak.

You can do all of those things and more in one amazing Asian country. That country is China. Come along to learn more about this fascinating country.

Your Passport to China

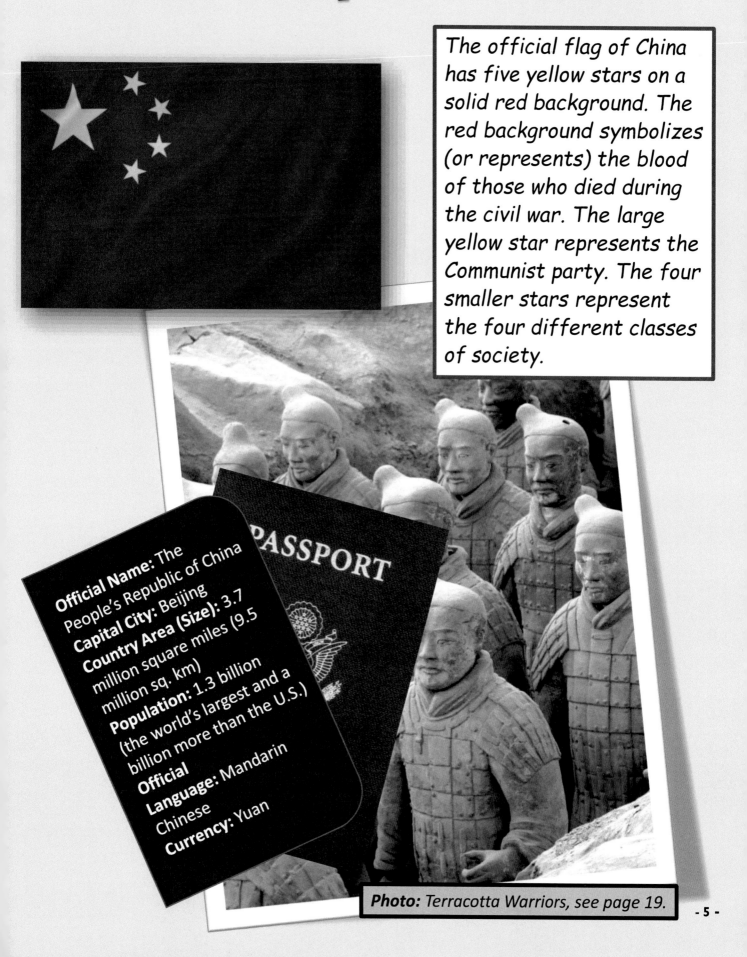

The official flag of China has five yellow stars on a solid red background. The red background symbolizes (or represents) the blood of those who died during the civil war. The large yellow star represents the Communist party. The four smaller stars represent the four different classes of society.

Official Name: The People's Republic of China
Capital City: Beijing
Country Area (Size): 3.7 million square miles (9.5 million sq. km)
Population: 1.3 billion (the world's largest and a billion more than the U.S.)
Official Language: Mandarin Chinese
Currency: Yuan

Photo: Terracotta Warriors, see page 19.

Where in the World Is China?

China is bordered by 14 Asian countries. How many can you find on the map?

CHINA IS A COUNTRY IN ASIA. It is bordered by the Pacific Ocean on its east coast and the Gobi Desert to the north. In the west, there are many mountains, including Mount Everest, the tallest mountain in the world.

China is the fourth largest country in the world as far as land area. The three larger countries are Russia, Canada, and the United States.

Most of the people in China live along the east coast or near the Yangtze River. (Say: yang-see.) It is the third longest river in the world. It flows across the center of China.

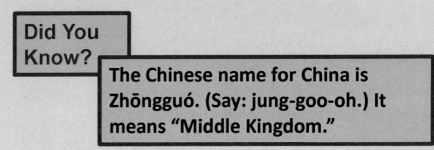

Did You Know?

The Chinese name for China is Zhōngguó. (Say: jung-goo-oh.) It means "Middle Kingdom."

A Brief History of China

China is one of the oldest **civilizations** in the world. It began more than 4,000 years ago when early Chinese people settled along the Yangtze and Yellow Rivers. Here are some important dates in Chinese history.

221 BC – 220 AD: People from the mainland settle on the island now known as Hong Kong.

221 BC: Qin Shi Huang [say: chin shee hwang] unifies (or joins together) all of China. He becomes the first Emperor.

1368 – 1644: The Ming **dynasty** rules China.

1421: Emperor Yongle of the Ming dynasty moves the capital of China to Beijing.

1842: The British Empire gains control of Hong Kong.

1912: The last emperor of China is overthrown; China becomes a **republic**.

1949: Mao Zedong (say: mow zuh-dung), also called Mao Tse-tung, becomes head of the **Communist Party** and establishes the People's Republic of China.

1976: Mao dies.

1997: China regains control of Hong Kong.

2008: Beijing hosts the Olympics.

7 Fun Facts About China

1 Some people think the number 13 is unlucky. In China, however, the number 4 is considered unlucky. (You won't find 4 on the number pad of most elevators.) So why is 4 considered unlucky? The pronunciation of the number 4 sounds like the Chinese character for death.

2 In the U.S. and other parts of the world, young brides often wear a white wedding dress. In China, they wear red. It is considered a lucky color.

3 More rice grows in China than anywhere else in the world.

4 The biggest dam in the world is on the Yangtze River. It's called the Three Gorges Dam.

5 China was the first country in the world to use paper money.

6 The oldest printed book in history is titled "The Diamond Sūtra." It was printed in China.

7 The Yangtze River is the third longest river in the world (after the Amazon and the Nile). It flows 3,915 miles (6,300 km). The longest river in the U.S., by the way, is the Missouri River. It flows 2,540 miles (4,087 km).

Photo: The Great Wall

How to Speak Chinese

MOST PEOPLE IN CHINA speak Mandarin Chinese. Mandarin Chinese doesn't have an alphabet. It is written with symbols. These symbols are called Chinese characters.

There are more than 100,000 Chinese characters. Imagine: 100,000! But don't worry. You only need to know about 2,000 of them in order to read and write basic stuff.

What is your name?

Nin gui xing?
(neen gway sing)

Hello

Nin hao
(neen how)

My name is [your name]

Wo jiao [your name]
(who jee-ow [your name])

Wow, that's so cool!

Hao bang ah!
(how bahng ah)

Friend

Pengyou
(pung-yoh)

You're welcome

Bu yong ke qi
(boo yong ke chi)

Thank you

Xie xie
(syeh syeh)

Goodbye

Zai jian
(zi-jee-an)

Photo: *Chinese style sailboat in Hong Kong*

Chinese Inventions

DO YOU ENJOY watching fireworks on the 4th of July? Or flying kites on a windy spring day? Or eating noodles of all kinds? If so, you have the ancient Chinese to thank. They invented all of these things and much more. Here are some of their inventions.

The world's first abacus

The Umbrella

The Compass

The wheelbarrow

Gun powder

Paper and printing

And, yes, even toilet paper. (Back then, it was used only by emperors.)

THERE IS ONE OTHER THING that the ancient Chinese invented. Can you guess what it is? You're right. Chopsticks.

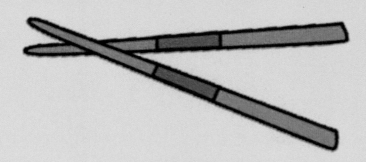

When they were first invented – oh, about 4,000 years ago – they were used mainly for cooking. The long, thin sticks could reach deep into pots of boiling water.

But around 500 to 400 AD, the Chinese began to use chopsticks to eat with. Food at the time was usually chopped up into small pieces. Chopsticks were the perfect means for picking up these small bites.

The Great Wall of China

ONE OF THE MOST FAMOUS places in the world is located in China. What is it? The Great Wall of China.

For years, experts said the wall was "only" 5,500 miles (8,850 km) long. But recently, China announced that the Great Wall extends 13,170 miles (21,196 km). If it were stretched out straight, it would go more than half-way around the earth!

Photo: The Great Wall of China

Actually, the Great Wall of China should probably be called the Great Double Wall. That's because it is actually two walls that run **parallel** to each other. They are about 15 feet (4.5 m) wide on average and about 35 feet (10.6 m) tall.

The wall was started by China's first emperor Qin in the third century BC. It was meant to keep invaders from the north from getting into the country. It included many watch towers. Soldiers who guarded the wall lived in the watchtowers.

The Giant Panda

EVERYBODY LOVES THE GIANT PANDA. It's about the cutest wild animal there is, right?

But did you know that the panda is found in the wild only in China. It lives in the mountains of central China.

Pandas can usually be found in thick bamboo forests. They love to eat the leaves of the evergreen plant. In fact, they eat as much as 20 to 40 pounds (9 to 18 kg) of bamboo each day.

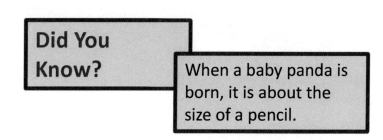

Did You Know?

When a baby panda is born, it is about the size of a pencil.

Sadly, the beautiful giant panda bears are **endangered.** That's because their natural habitat is slowly being destroyed. Their forests are being cleared for development and building or for farming. Today, scientists estimate that there are only about 1,000 pandas in the wild.

With its black eye patches and huge paws, the giant panda is recognized and loved by people all over the world.

The Forbidden City

Photo: *The throne in the Palace of Heavenly Purity in the Forbidden City.*

FOR HUNDREDS OF YEARS, the emperors of China lived in a palace complex known as the Forbidden City in Beijing. It was called the Forbidden City because ordinary people were not allowed in without special permission.

The Forbidden City was a huge complex with nearly 10,000 rooms. The complex was surrounded by a moat 170 feet (52 m) wide. That's about half as long as a football field.

The Forbidden City was started in the early 1400s and took about 15 years to build. Emperors and their families lived there until 1911.

Today, the Forbidden City is probably China's most well-known museum. Every year, thousands of kids from all over the world visit it.

The Forbidden City has at least 1,000 buildings, including palaces, temples, as well as rivers, parks and lakes.

Photo: *The Hall of Supreme Harmony is the largest hall in the Forbidden City.*

Confucius

AROUND 2,500 YEARS AGO, there was a famous teacher and **philosopher** in China. His name was Confucius. (Say: conn-FYU-shuss.) He taught people the importance of many different things, including education and kindness and **morality**. He had many strict rules about behavior. His teachings had great influence on the people of ancient China.

Confucius had many sayings and ideas that are important even today. Here is just one of them. "*Respect yourself and others will respect you.*"

The Terra-Cotta Army

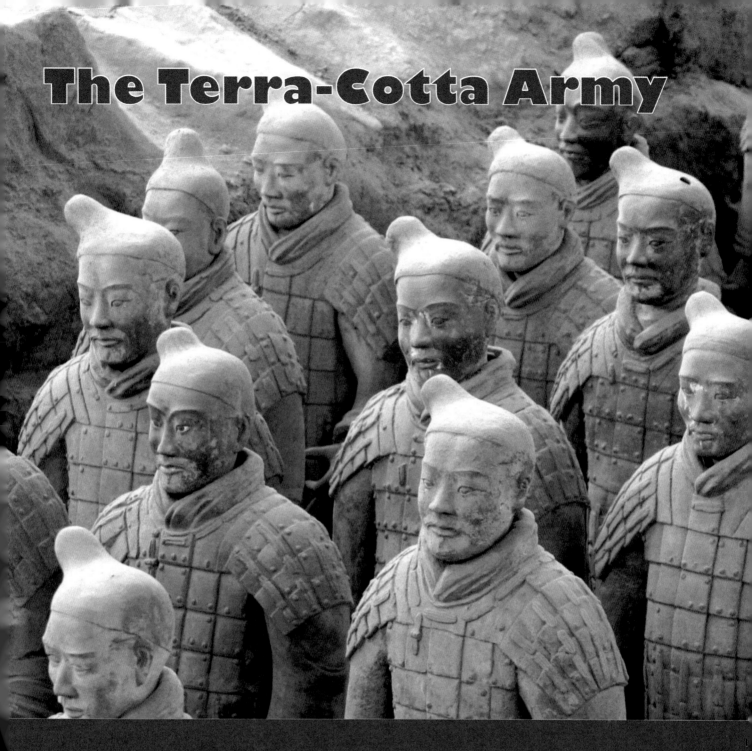

A TOTAL OF 8,000 life-size clay soldiers stand guard around the tomb of the Emperor Qin, who died in 210 BC. Their purpose is to protect the emperor in the **afterlife**. It took 37 years to make this "army." More than 700,000 people worked on the project.

No two figures out of the 8,000 are exactly alike. Each face of the 8,000 statues is slightly different.

Fun Facts About the Big Cities of China

Photo: Wangfujing Street in Beijing

CHINA HAS MANY BIG, MORDERN CITIES. They are very much like any big city in the U.S. or around the world. There are skyscrapers, busy streets, and millions of people. Here are some fun facts about three famous cities in China.

Beijing

Photo: National Stadium

Beijing is the capital of China. It has 21 million people. It is also the educational center of China. More than 500 universities are in Beijing.

The centerpiece of the 2008 Summer Olympics was the Beijing National Stadium. Its nickname is "The Bird's Nest" because of its nest-like skeletal structure.

Fun Fact: People in Beijing love to ride bicycles. It is a popular (and easy) way to get around town.

Shanghai

Photo: Pjt56@gmx.net

Shanghai is at the mouth of the Yangtze River, and an important business center of China. It is China's largest city in terms of population (and the 8th largest in the world). It has 23 million people. The largest city in the U.S. – New York City -- has 20 million people. Los Angeles has 15 million.

Fun Fact: Shanghai means "City on the Sea."

Hong Kong

Photo: Hong Kong Island north coast, Victoria Harbour, and Kowlon in Hong Kong.

Hong Kong is officially known as the Hong Kong Special Administrative Region of the People's Republic of China. It is one of the richest places in the world. Starting in 1842, Hong Kong was a British **colony**. It became part of China in 1997.

Fun Fact: Hong Kong in Chinese means "**fragrant** port."

Life in China Today

Photo: *Li River in Guangxi*

WHAT IS LIFE LIKE in China today? In many ways, it's like life in the United States. In the big cities, there are large supermarkets and department stores. There are even Walmart stores.

In the villages, there are many small, local markets. People come to these markets not only to shop but to socialize and visit with friends as well.

Whether in the city or the village, family life is very important in China. Often, grandparents, parents, and children all share the same house. Young people often live at home until they get married.

Education in China

Photo: *A student practices writing Chinese characters*

JUST LIKE KIDS in the United States, kids in China go to school. They study many of the same subjects as you do, including language and math. They also study English starting in first grade.

But kids in China also have classes in moral education. They study what it means to be a good citizen and how to maintain good moral values.

Games Kids Play:
Catch the Dragon

WANT TO PLAY a fun Chinese game? Try Catch the Dragon. Start by getting a large group together. Everyone lines up. The person in front of the line is the Dragon's head. The person at the end of the line is the Dragon's tail. All of the players between the Dragon's head and the Dragon's tail place their two hands on the shoulders of the person directly in front of them.

The goal is for the Dragon's head to tag the Dragon's tail. This is hard, though, since the line must stay connected. At the same time, the players behind the Dragon's head try to keep it from catching the Dragon's tail.

When the dragon's head catches the dragon's tail, the head becomes the tail and the player who is next in line becomes the dragon's head. Fun!

The Chinese Calendar

THE TRADITIONAl CHINESE CALENDAR is divided into 12 months or one year. Each year is associated with (or named after) a particular animal. For example, 2017 is the Year of the Rooster.

According to Chinese legend, each animal has certain traits or characteristics. A rooster, for example, crows at the same time every morning. It is very punctual. A person born in the Year of the Rooster would also be very punctual, according to Chinese custom.

Rat: 2008

Ox: 2009

Tiger: 2010

Rabbit: 2011

Dragon: 2012

Snake: 2013

Horse: 2014

Goat: 2015

Monkey: 2016

Rooster: 2017

Dog: 2018

Pig: 2019

What's to Eat?
Food in China

WHEN YOU THINK of Chinese food, you probably think of chow mein, spring rolls, or maybe sweet and sour pork. And those are all popular dishes in China.

But there are many other favorite foods in China that you may not have heard of. Here are three of them.

Congee: A soupy rice porridge that may be eaten at any time of day; it often includes fish, yams, or beans. ➡

Jiaozi (say jowzuh): Dumplings filled with meat, fish, or vegetables; they may be steamed, boiled or fried. It's a special dish especially for the Chinese New Year.

Dim sum: Dim sum is a general name for a whole variety of small Chinese dishes, including small <u>dumplings</u>, won tons, and <u>egg rolls</u>, and other foods. ➡

Did You Know?

A Chinese meal usually includes soup, dumplings, and plenty of rice or noodles.

Chinese Festivals

CHINESE LOVE CELEBRATIONS and festivals.

The largest celebration each year – and the most important one for the Chinese people -- is the Spring Festival. That's when the Chinese New Year is celebrated. Families members get together to celebrate.

In the U.S. the new year always falls on January 1. The date of the Chinese New Year is different each year. It falls between the end of January and the beginning of February.

Chinese people decorate their houses with mandarin trees during the Spring Festival. There's no Santa Claus or presents in China. But the children do get Red Envelopes, which contain money – lucky money.

Chinese Festivals

THE DRAGON BOAT FESTIVAL is usually held in June in memory of one of China's earliest poets named Qu Yuan. He drowned himself in 278 BC. Boats decorated to look like colorful dragons take part in an exciting race. The races are a symbol of the attempts to rescue and recover the body of Qu Yuan.

Chinese Festivals

The Lantern Festival is held each year throughout the country in February or March. Colorful lanterns of various sizes and shapes are hung in the streets.

National Day: This day celebrates the founding of the People's Republic of China (PRC) in 1949. The weeklong holiday begins October 1 each year and includes fireworks, concerts, and other festivities.

Glossary

Afterlife: Life after death; a life that some people believe exists after death.

Civilization: An advanced state of development of a society

Colony: A place where a group of people come to settle which is under control by a distant country.

Communist Party: A political party that supports communism.

Dynasty: A series of rulers from the same family.

Emperor: The male ruler of an empire.

Fragrant: Having a pleasant or nice smell.'

Parallel: Two things that run or lie in the same direction and are the same distance apart at all points.

Philosopher: One who studies ideas about the nature of life and truth.

Punctual: Prompt; on time.

Sovereign (adj.): Having an independent government.

Symbolize: To represent; to serve as a representation of something.

Virtue: Goodness; right action or thoughts; morally good behavior or character.

For Beginning Readers
The Elephant Picture Book

Curious Kids Press

The Elephant Picture Book

With original photography of the elephants at Boon Lott's Elephant Sanctuary in Thailand.

Ages 4-7

By Jack L. Roberts
With Photography by Michael Owens

Available as E-book or Print Edition!

Other Books from Curious Kids Press

www.curiouskidspress.com

PlanetKids Series (ages 7-9)

PlanetKids: Ancient Egypt

PlanetKids: Australia

PlanetKids: Costa Rica

PlanetKids: France

PlanetKids: Kenya

PlanetKids: Thailand

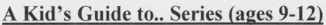

A Kid's Guide to.. Series (ages 9-12)

A Kid's Guide to Ancient Egypt

A Kid's Guide to Australia

A Kid's Guide to China

A Kid's Guide to Costa Rica

A Kid's Guide to France

A Kid's Guide to Kenya

A Kid's Guide to Thailand

Other CKP eBooks for Kids

A Kid's Guide to
CHiNa
For Parents and Teachers

About This Book

A Kid's Guide to . . . is an engaging, easy-to-read e-book series that provides an exciting adventure into fascinating countries and cultures around the world for young readers. Each book focuses on one country and includes colorful photographs, informational charts and graphs, and quirky and bizarre "Did You Know" facts, all designed to bring the country and its people to life. Designed primarily for recreational, high-interest reading, the informational text series is also a great resource for students to use to research geography topics or writing assignments.

About the Reading Level

A Kid's Guide to . . . is an informational text series designed for kids n grades 4 to 6, ages 9 to 12. For some young readers, the series will provide new reading challenges based on the vocabulary and sentence structure. For other readers, the series will reinforce reading skills already achieved. While for still other readers, the series text will match their current skill level, regardless of age or grade level.

About the Author

Jack L. Roberts began his career in educational publishing at Children's Television Workshop (now Sesame Workshop), where he was Senior Editor of The Sesame Street/Electric Company Reading Kits. Later, at Scholastic Inc., he was the founding editor of a high-interest/low-reading level magazine for middle school students. Roberts is the author of more than a dozen biographies and other non-fiction titles for young readers, published by Scholastic Inc., the Lerner Publishing Group, and Benchmark Education. More recently, he was the co-founder of WordTeasers, an educational series of card decks designed to help kids of all ages improve their vocabulary through "conversation, not memorization."

Made in the USA
Middletown, DE
03 April 2020

87856113R00022